THE
PASSION
WITHIN

~~~~

A Collection of Poems
And Short Stories
With an Urban Touch

Written and Compiled by RM Green
Also Featuring the Works of:

Terance Williams * Noah Travis * Felecia Trotter
Jason Tucker * Timothy Hollins

THE PASSION WITHIN

Safe Haven Publishing Company
P.O. Box 6841
Beaufort, SC 29903

ISBN-13: 978-0-6151-5561-6

Reviews for RM Green and *'The Passion Within'...*

"Ms. Green is a rare talent, she has the ability to take the mundane melodrama of everyday life and breath new life into it. Her writing conveys a passion for literature. Her poetry is simply brilliant, colorfully scripted, and lyrically flowing. She has a keen understanding of word artistry and paints scenes that capture the mind and unleash the emotions. Using her pen she is able to weave a tapestry of sight, sound, taste, and feelings into every masterpiece she creates. I would recommend her work to anyone looking to not just read poetry but rather to experience word art. "

Dr. Tyan J. Byrd Sr. PhD.,
Author of *'FYRE & ICE'*

"RM Green is an author that gives you reality, action, suspense and a page-turner in her 'EVERYBODY PLAYZ THE FOOL' series...she has talent that is out of this world...."

Claudia Brown-Mosley, author of *'I CAN HAVE MY CAKE AND EAT IT TOO...'*

"RM Green concocts stories that include real-life situations and high dramatization. She takes the time to develop her characters so that the reader can relate to them. Her work stands in a category of it's own. Reading RM Green's work, whether it's a story or a poem, will touch on your emotions and make you remember. That's what good writing is all about. "

Teresa D. Patterson, Author of *'IT'S YOUR WORLD, BLACK GIRL!'*

"RM Green's skills is pure flawlessness in every way, the depth in her words are very captivating--- She can make the ink-dotted invisible lines behind each letter appear in full view... And the most impressive thing about her is how she lets her mind and pen share the same flow. RM Green is just simply amazing..."

Vanesso Louis, Author and Poet

First and Foremost, I dedicate this book to
GOD,
Without Whom NOTHING is possible!!

~~~~~

I further dedicate this book to my Grandmother,
Eleanor Brown,
March 19, 1911 - February 25, 2006

Who was truly the light of my life, or as the Bette Midler song goes, *"The wind beneath my wings"*.

I will always love you, Ma... I Miss You!!

This first poem is dedicated to my grandmother, who raised me, nurtured me, and was truly my guiding light and best friend all my life until she closed her eyes for the final time on February 25, 2006. I wrote this poem through my tears of grief, which reopened the floodgates of my passion for writing again after 14 years. It is because of the lesson she taught me in death - to live my dreams before it is too late - that I write.

MY HEART'S SONG

She was my guiding light in times of darkness,
My rock when I was devoid of strength,
Wisdom when I had no clue.
Understanding when I performed the unexpected
And encouragement when fear reared its ugly head.

I miss the sound of her laughter,
And the love that poured from her lips with each word she spoke.
She lived a life full of God's unconditional love
An angel, my angel, here on earth,

I miss the touch of her still baby-soft skin
That 94 years on this earth did not weather
I miss asking her if she needed anything
Because I certainly needed her caring words
To guide me, lift me, and carry me through my day.

It has been a little while now that she has gone to meet the Creator,
The one who allowed me to have her in my life
And who allowed her to nurture me
To become the person you now see.

I feel bittersweet sorrow
Knowing she is free and no longer in pain
And is united with God as she is so entitled.
The memories of her make me smile, but
The pain I feel is everlasting.

Just know that when all is said and done
She was, is and will forever be
My Heart's Song.

~~~

In Loving Memory of Eleanor Brown, My Grandmother
March 19, 1911 - February 25, 2006

Dedicated to the Black Man... BECAUSE I Love You So...

BECAUSE

Because you are strong, yet gentle...
Because you are proud, yet humble...
Because you are so wise, yet so young...
Because you are genuine to the core.

Because you have ideals that are unshakable
Because you have faith that is unbreakable.
Because you exhibit and demand respect
Because you feel more deeply than most would ever expect.

Because you are fair and strive for peace,
Because you adore your heritage, vow to teach
Because our ancestors were enslaved
And your heart and spirit is enraged
That society has raped us, depraved
Our history is rich, and has engaged
Upon the journey to our rightful stage
Among the Royalty of dominion, rebuilding our kingdoms
To future dominance and total freedom!

Because you seek to lift the hearts of many
Because you possess charm, its powers uncanny
Because, devoted father, all children you love and protect
Because you are a REAL MAN, deserving of love, history reflects ...

Is why you are...
My Hero.

For Single Moms Everywhere...

<u>Sometimes I Cry</u>

Sometimes I cry, late at night
When I'm all alone, no one to hold me tight
Wondering what is my purpose, by and by
And if it makes much difference whether I live or die?

As I struggle along, working each day
It seems that I'm not making much headway.
It is only for my children that I strive
To keep pushing on, and stay alive.

The pain I have suffered throughout my life
Keeps playing through my mind, the stress and strife.
Why is this emptiness constantly eating at me
With no end in sight; it just won't let me be.

Abuse from the hands of one I had once loved so dear
Had me walking on eggshells, living in fear.
The scars from such I still bear to this day
And even after fifteen years, they still haven't gone away.

Even now, when my family holds things from the past
Against me, causing me to feel like an outcast
All I can do is recoil in my soul and retreat
To my neutral corner, and lick my wounds in defeat.

What keeps me going today is the look in my children's eyes,
Who love me unconditionally, as if I'm some great prize.
I'm just a Mom, who tries to give them more than
I had, without much help from family, or from some man.

The pressure to succeed seems so overbearing
And doing this all alone takes its toll on my very being.
To those who may be weaker, this life isn't worth the fight
As for me, I still stand strong so this is why

Sometimes I Cry...

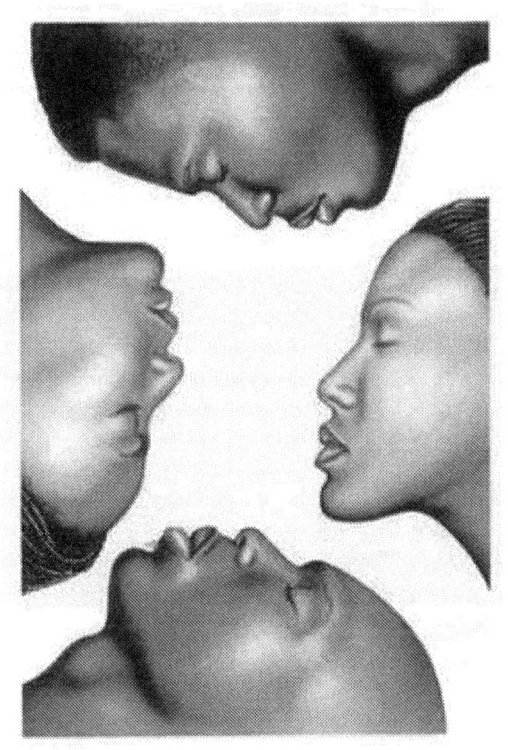

SAFE HAVEN

When I am feeling depressed
And stressed because I cannot
Give my children what they need or crave,
I need a safe haven
To allow me to scream in my silence.

When my work overcomes me,
Long hours toiling, striving,
Making that paper to feed and house my family,
I need a safe haven
To free my mind, rejuvenate my purpose.

When my body craves a man's touch,
And there is none forthcoming
Because the one I love is far from me,
I need a safe haven
To release my loins from want and need.

When I need a friend
To encourage me to press on,
Realize my dream, accomplish my goals,
You are my safe haven
To regroup, gather the strength to proceed.

When you need to cry and confess
That while strong and confident on the outside
The child inside seeks comfort and reassurance,
I am your safe haven
To allow the child to cry, receive the love it deserves.

A safe haven judges not,
Tells nothing and respects always.
It protects, lets one be who they truly are,
Freely and completely, no strings attached.
It envelops the heart and cleanses the soul.

When the world beats us down
With societal rules, family squabbles,
Financial burdens, disease and life challenges,
Just when you think there's no hope, only despair,
Know that God is the Safest Haven of all.

Magic Happens Online for Many of Us…

<u>Soul Behind The Eye</u>

Searching through a maze
Of images on a screen
I freeze at the sight of the one
That momentarily stilled my pulse.

The sight of an eye
Gazing silently at me
Spoke to my soul and
Penetrated my being

With such force I yearned to reach out
And comfort his hurt, erase his suffering,
Protect and hold his sensitive spirit,
And Love his Pain away.

Behind the eye I saw an aching soul,
Which housed a tender, passionate heart
Undeserving of the abuse witnessed and felt
By the child that dwelled within.

Strong, dominant leader of men he became,
A being of strong character and analytical
Intelligence, father of two men-children, leader
Protector of family, fruit of his loins.

Women recognize the potency of his power,
Awe at the gentleness nestled within his strength,
Swoon at the sound of his commanding voice,
Quiver at the magnificence of his masculine body.

Brave enough to stand for his beliefs,
Always determined to fight for what's right,
Unquenchable knowledge seeker, teacher and friend
Loyalty governs his essence to the bitter end.

I witness the makeup of a man
Who gripped my heart with the image of an eye,
The trials and scars I spot through the eye's pane
Of whom I vow to love the pain away.

I, as well as many living in this country, are part Native American. My Native American ancestry is of the Shinnecock Nation of Long Island, New York, where several of my family members still serve on the reservation as council members and chiefs, and hold traditional celebrations during regular powwows. These next two pieces are borne out of a reflection of that heritage within me, and have previously been published in Autumn Leaves, a Native American online publication.

Shinnecock Dreams

Bronze hills against powder blue skies,
Azure waters run along stone strewn land,
Majestic pines and mighty oaks
Proudly hold their mighty branches high,
To house delicate nests brimming with new life.

Scarlet petals on long jade stems
Vividly unfurl with amazing grace,
Golden rays and white whispers,
Scattered in bunches upon the deep brown earth
Take in nourishing energy from the sun.

Gentle breezes sift through forest leaves
And gently kiss the bronzed cheek
Of the child beneath who drinks in
The glory of God's magnificent earth,
Dark eyes full of admiration and wonder.

Here, peace and joy enfold him,
Calms his heart, feeding his imagination
With animated images of dancing sparrows
Flying high in the Shinnecock sky,
Welcoming the child's marvel in the miracle of life.

In the distance snowcapped mountains reign,
As the clouds hug the rugged surface
And the falling water carves its name,
So does the aura of earth's beauty
Define nature as being one with God.

Copyright @2006, by RM Green

WARRIOR LOVE

Sun bronzed skin
and powerful build
swathes a tender heart
sweet as honey and fragile as glass
yearning to taste the sweet nectar of her kiss

Her love within burns bright
as the sun across the glistening sky.
Eyes full of adoration and pride
Relish the contours of his body
And the gentle vigor of his touch.

Virgin desire burning deep within,
Passions devour them in sweet, sultry bliss,
Reaching the pinnacle of erotic rapture
Merging their essence as one,
drowning them in the throes of ecstasy.

Warrior and Squaw both now soar,
Wild, majestic and free,
Like great birds of prey,
Souls and hearts entwined in regal stance
Awash in the elixir of forever love.

These next pieces describe Love and Passion... of a different kind!

VALENTINE SWEETS

Your lips,
succulent and sweet
as melon gumdrops,
glistening with sugary dew.

Your kiss,
nectar of your essence
devours my soul, and
drinks of my life breath within.

Your touch
electrifies my warm skin,
tenderizes my heart,
envelops me with desire for...

Your body,
pressed naked against mine
fire mounting within our loins,
marinating our juices, tasting passion.

Chocolate candy
smooth, silky and rigid,
simmering with vanilla cream
to release within my cotton candy folds.

Savory brown gravy
poured over my cinnamon buns,
creates a culinary sensation when
your hot chocolate explodes within my éclair.

Your love,
charming and tender as God above
encases my heart and spirit,
everlasting as precious diamonds, and true.

Tapestry of Desire

I look into your eyes...
While circling the inside of your thighs
With the sultry touch of my finger
Moving my hand ever so close to growing fire.

I kiss your candy lips
As I lightly outline your manhood
Feeling you grow larger, and harder
At my wanting touch

We kiss softly and sweetly
As our passion within grows
Aah... but wait!
If you touch me. . I will stop!

I tell you to relax,
Keep your hands beside you
I want you to close your eyes, keep still
Just FEEL what I do to you

Feel me tonguing your nipples
As I caress your precious sacs within my grasp
Gently squeezing, caressing in my fingers
I delight watching your manhood stiffen and dance

Within the cloth of your boxers
The tip lightly staining the fabric
I feel the desire building within you.
Until I uncover the wonders of your magnificent member

I pull off your boxers
With my teeth and tongue
As you watch me lick my chocolate lollipop
To get to taste its creamy center.

NO! You can't touch me, I'll stop
I want to tease you, please you, take you deeper
Inside my mouth, suckle you longer, sweeter
My hands feel the sacs tighten...ready to explode...

I tell you I want to drink you up...
Taste your salty sweet juices
Flow down the back of my throat
As I drain every ounce of you

Your sultry sounds and strong, sexy body
Ignites a chain reaction in my loins
I explode into a sea of passion juices...
And await thee for more...

Copyright @2006, RM Green

This next poem was inspired by many who live and die by their word and bond - L.A. Gang members, particularly members of the notorious Crips and Bloods. There is a much deeper truth to Bloods and Crips than what the world has come to know through Hollywood movies and rappers. What the vast majority of our society DOES NOT know is that in Los Angeles, being a gang member for many is a WAY OF LIFE, and many are ordinary citizens just like you and I. These men grew up in gangs, and their fathers, grandfathers, uncles and brothers were also gang members. They also work, and are brick masons, electricians, business owners, etc., and some are even lawyers and professionals who hold bachelors and/or doctorate degrees. Many do NOT hurt and kill others, and to PROTECT and RESPECT are their mottos. I DO NOT carry an affiliation with any particular L.A. Gang, or any other gang for that matter. I just learned much about the lifestyle through a friend who happens to have been a Blood at one point in his life, so I write this from that perspective. However, these words can be applied to either or ALL. This tribute is for them...

HEART OF A BLOOD

Men of strong conviction and
protectors of those they love,
Bloods are their Brother's keeper
all the way until the bitter end.

They walk down these LA Streets
reppin' their 'hood with menacing glances
against intruders, uninvited threats,
disrespectful others, discipline to dispense.

Their hearts beat the same red blood
that flows though all our veins,
they seek the same love we all need,
not to live in violence and die in vain.

Feelings within they hide from view,
the pain they bear no one can see.
Tears they cry inside their souls
are wiped away by their strength & pride.

Fathers, brothers, sons and uncles,
teachers, preachers, electricians and welders,
strong, dominant, powerful and true warriors,
they are family, Bloods, one and all.

All they want is to find true love,
a sense of belonging, peace within.
Of all the things of value here on earth,
the Heart of a Blood is most precious of all.

Copyright @2006, RM Green

Short Stories
(Book Excerpts)
By
RM Green,
Author of the novel,
'SHE COULD HEAR THE SILENCE'

'SHE COULD HEAR THE SILENCE'
Part V - SIMONE
(Short Story - Excerpt #1 from the upcoming novel by RM Green)

Simone could really identify with Janae about making it on her own in spite of the fact that her ex-husband tried to set her up to fail. He had underestimated her. Janae is a strong and intelligent woman who doesn't let life's twists and turns get her down for long – she is a fighter and survivor. Simone pictured herself being much the same way.

Alexis' father has had almost no interaction with their daughter at all, and basically abandoned Simone after she told him she was pregnant. She raised her daughter alone through it all - living with various family members while having little or no money, to working and earning her college degree in Humanities. Eventually she went to real estate school and became a licensed property manager, got her own apartment, then finally becoming a real estate agent and buying her own home. She accomplished what she wanted to do and raised Alexis, an extremely bright, 13-year-old straight–A student who never gave Simone a minute of trouble, by herself. She knows she has been blessed.

However, almost 18 months ago, Alexis' father Reggie had come back into their lives. He begged for another chance to reconnect with her and their daughter. Simone had rarely dated and she felt she needed to give him a chance to get to know their daughter, and do something for her for once in his life. He seemed to have a genuine interest in them, had finally grown up and was ready to take on his responsibilities as a father.

"I never knew how much I really loved you and missed you until I messed around and lost you," Reggie had pleaded with Simone. "I missed out on seeing my baby grow up, and now I want to have the chance to connect with her, to be in her life."

"I don't know if I will ever be able to trust you, Reggie. You disappeared from our lives almost as soon as I told you I was pregnant. And I have raised her myself for almost 14 years now. I am not going to allow you to be a part-time father; Alexis deserves better than that," said Simone firmly. "You are either in this for the long haul, or don't bother coming in our lives, especially HER life, at all!"

"Please Simone, please let me come back, Boo. I have always loved you and you will see that I have changed. I am finally ready to be a father, a real daddy, to my little girl", Reggie pleaded again, and finally convinced Simone he was sincere. She introduced him to their daughter, who at first was in shock, but warmed up to him quickly, absolutely delighted to finally have a daddy. After about a month or so, she let him move in.

Simone had to admit she still carried a torch for him, even after all she had done and gone through all by herself. She remembered what a good lover he was, and he surely reminded her during their first night together again – the sex was mind-boggling as always. Her body longed for a man's touch once again, and this release felt GOOD, so long overdue she literally experienced the most intense orgasm of her life. Besides, it was so nice to have a man around after so long alone.

This little family reunion only lasted about 3 months, after which Reggie did what Reggie does best – disappear. Simone was heartbroken again, however their daughter was absolutely devastated. She'd finally had the dad – HER DAD – in her life that she had craved so much in her young life, only for her elation to be gone in a flash. Simone comforted Alexis as best she could, had gotten them both into counseling, and she seemed to be coping well now. However she still worries about how her daughter is REALLY doing in the back of her mind.

She still hasn't told her daughter about last week.

She had been reading the newspaper during lunch at the office when something caught her eye. She noticed 'Reginald Montague' - Reggie's name - listed in the obituaries, and read the entry. *Oh my God, he's dead!* Simone exclaimed to herself. Grief, shock and disbelief began to well inside her. She wanted to make sure to attend the wake, which the newspaper stated was to be held later that evening.

When she arrived, there was a small gathering of people milling around the funeral home outside. She went in and found the room where Reggie's body was laid out.

Reggie looked very peaceful, as if he were sleeping, but it was apparent he had been very sick and lost a lot of weight. She also noticed that Reggie had a rather large and familiar-looking reddish-brown spot on his right cheek. She didn't recognize anyone at the wake, so she asked the funeral home secretary what he had died from.

"The official cause of death is listed as pneumonia on the death certificate, which was a direct complication of the rare form of cancer he suffered from. AIDS patients often acquire this type of cancer," said the secretary.

Simone felt as though a ton of bricks had just hit her. AIDS? *He died of AIDS?!?* She suddenly felt very sick to her stomach.

"Thank you," Simone said, and then turned to walk out into the cool night air as she left the funeral home. She had recently noticed a small brown spot, similar to the one she had just seen on Reggie, on her chest just below her right collarbone.

She could hear the silence roaring through her head, as the fear, dread and stark reality of her situation began to take shape in her mind.

Would she be around to see Alexis grow up? She put her head in her hands and wept.

'SHE COULD HEAR THE SILENCE'
Part III, SARAH
(Excerpt #2 from the upcoming novel by RM Green)

When Sarah and Jason first got together, they pictured themselves as the 'neo couple', a break away from the traditional household makeup. Sarah, being the top rising executive at her advertising firm servicing new accounts, would work and bring home the lion's share of the bacon. Jason, being a master at pottery – he made some incredible pieces that sold almost instantly when he would sell them at various galleries, festivals, craft shows and flea markets in the DC area - was also a brilliant watercolor artist, and it was agreed he would stay home to perfect his craft and keep house.

They saw nothing wrong with this arrangement and Sarah would proudly boast that Jason was a 'proud househusband'. This fed her desire to forge ahead in her career and 'break the glass ceiling', whereas he was free to use his artistic talents to make and sell his wares, along with giving him security as he attempted to move past the 'starving artist' stage and get real critical acclaim for his pieces. His plan was to eventually be at least an equal contributor to the family pocketbook.

Jason is an extremely handsome human creation, almost a dead-ringer for the singer Maxwell, with his strong chiseled features, tan skin and curly/nappy hair worn slightly long and natural. The way he walks is a sight to behold – sensuous, strong and confident, not cocky. However, unlike Maxwell, Jason can NOT hold a tune if you gave it to him in a bucket. He is talented in many other ways, and it is in those areas Sarah revels in him.

He knows how to make REAL love to her, and make her feel like a woman – a REAL woman, the way a woman should feel.

On a typical evening, they would sit, talk and laugh for hours, curled up on the couch or in the bed, after enjoying a nice dinner. They shared an incredibly strong bond and once they stopped talking and began looking dreamily into each other's eyes, the electricity in their bodies seemed to unknowingly draw them closer, until they kissed softly at first, licking and sucking each other's lips gently yet passionately, until they fell into a deep passionate kiss that sets their bodies on fire.

Jason would slip one hand under her white silk blouse and find that she wasn't wearing a bra, and her nipples would stand erect. He is on top of her in an instant, kissing her, moving his fingers between her legs, feeling her wetness beneath her black skirt as he pressed his body against hers and made her feel his male hardness against her belly. His fingers would brush against her clit ever so slightly, and the sensation would make her back arch as moans slip from her lips. He would continue to gently stimulate her slippery clit, it felt SO GOOD to her!

He would then open her blouse and move his sweet lips to her breasts, gently suckling and pulling on her super-sensitive nipples with his lips and tongue – he KNEW how sensitive her nipples were and this excited him even more. Jason would feel Sarah's body begin to tremble as he brought her closer to climax – her nipples were just that sensitive! His lips and tongue would find their way down her stomach, to her navel, to her thighs before they find her clit. As he would begin licking and sucking on it, he would feel her clit begin to harden and throb in his mouth as he feels her cum flow across his lips and down his chin. He would grab and hold tightly but tenderly to her hips as her body trembled and rocked in waves with each successive orgasm, as whimpers and moans escaped from deep within her throat… and made sure to end the night with them both in sheer bliss.

Sarah has no doubt that he loves her. He's always been loyal and faithful, and as much as her job keeps her away and on the go, there has never been a hint of unfaithfulness from him, ever – and he has always been an AMAZING lover. He's a great friend, and is straight up with her at all times. He is not afraid to tell her that she's wrong when she is wrong, and defend her and be her biggest ally when she's right. Any suggestions he makes regarding her is always in her best interests, even when he knows she doesn't want to hear it.

"You know you should not have shot Phaedra down like that, Boo," chided Jason. "She is just saying what is on most people's minds, they don't understand our stance when it comes to our household. And that's cool, people are entitled to their opinions."

"She basically called you a lazy bum, and that infuriated me! She of ALL people should understand non-traditional societal roles, if anyone does. Her own family barely speaks to her because of her sexual preferences – or variety thereof, I should say. THAT'S what got to me!" exclaimed Sarah, after relating last night's events to Jason the following day.

"I know it sounded as if she was being hypocritical, especially in light of her situation, but it is perfectly understandable. Society conditions everyone's ideals of what constitutes acceptable behavior to them. Just like her sexual preferences are not acceptable to YOU, our living arrangement is not acceptable to HER. You are being just as hypocritical assuming SHE should understand US. Do you get it now?" Jason remarked analytically.

"I never thought of it that way," she answered, suddenly enlightened.

"Could the fact that YOU could be the object of her affections cloud your judgment toward her in this respect as well? Hell, I sometimes wonder if I should be jealous of HER!" exclaimed Jason. "She has a full time job, is smart as hell being a college professor, and you wouldn't have to work so hard if you were with her. She's probably cute, too!"

Sarah just sat there, listened and said nothing, not very pleased with the way this conversation is going. Jason is still unaware of her growing displeasure with the current state of affairs, and this was nagging at the back of her mind. It seems he hasn't worked on his pottery in almost a year, he rarely cleans or cooks anymore, and his drinking has increased. At one time during their very early courtship, he would never even touch alcohol, which is one of the things he now lacks that originally attracted her to him.

She had defended Jason to Phaedra, but perhaps she had a point. Sarah was tired of working like a dog only to end up treading water. She was growing tired of working so hard and this arrangement was beginning to get old. Jason used to be so ambitious about his projects and getting them done to display and sell, but the fire seems to have been replaced by complacency. Her discontent would turn into resentment if she didn't do something about it now. *After three and a half years like this, would Jason be open to getting a job? At least part-time?* Sarah half-wondered, half-prayed.

"I am simply a starving artist who is desperately in love with you," Jason continued, looking at her adoringly. "That is all I can give you at this point, my undying love."

Sarah sat there for a moment, as if in deep thought, then cleared her throat. *OK, here it goes...* she thought to herself. *I must be honest and true to myself above all else..*

"Baby, I hate to say this, but perhaps Phaedra has a point," Sarah finally said.

"What?" Jason said, in almost a whisper, staring at her with bewilderment in his eyes. He was in shock and disbelief at her words.

"Sweetheart, I really haven't seen you do anything with your pottery or paints lately. You are such an incredible talent! Why are you letting it all go to waste?" she attempted to say affectionately, but the edge of her frustration seeped through. "Every day, when I come home, the house is a mess and I see you crumpled on a chair or on the sofa. I am at a loss wondering what you do here all day long. You have even taken to drinking now – what's up with THAT?"

Jason was speechless. Her words just cut through him like a knife, and she was slowly twisting the dagger through his heart. *Hadn't I always been there for her?* Jason thought to himself. *Hadn't I always been faithful to her, worshipped her like the Black Queen she is? Treated her as a Queen is supposed to be treated? Loved her as I have loved no other? Hadn't I been her humble and willing servant? How can she be so hypocritical and say these things to ME? And NOW, after I just bared my soul and thoughts to her?*

Jason is so crushed that he could barely stand any longer. His eyes glaze over, then well with tears. *Just when I am about to ask her the ultimate question, ready to finally give over my heart and soul to my one true love, I hear this from her...*

Sarah is watching him closely, and she cannot tell at this point exactly WHAT he is thinking or feeling. She DOES know – now – that she hurt him deeply, and she also knows she is scared as hell. She has NEVER seen him react this way – retreat and draw into a shell, tears streaming down his face, totally silent and in his own world. She remains silent, afraid to move or speak.

After a few silent moments, Jason finally seems to regain enough composure to turn and look her straight in the eye.

"I thought I was living a dream, and apparently I was. I thought that we were always on one accord, lived as one soul and I would have gladly given my life for you, in a heartbeat. You were right by my side, comforting me through the deaths of my parents and only brother in that car crash last year, and nursed me through much of my depression and despair. You were all I had, and I thanked God for you and our love. I still sat here when you were working, all alone, and thank the Father above for you – you would be home and be here, just for me. Of all the people on this earth, I thought YOU understood me, understood my needs, understood that I loved YOU – and only YOU – unconditionally, and that my life, my body and my soul was devoted only to you. I thought we defined our life and love on our terms, not anyone else's, DAMN what society dictates. I gave you pure, unadulterated and unabashed love and friendship. I tried to show you every day of my life, through honest and heartfelt words and deeds, how much I truly loved and appreciated you. How I would gladly kiss the ground you walked on, worship the air you breathed – you were my earth, my moon, my heart."

Then Jason stood up, and while wiping away his tears, and for the very first time since they have been together, his immense hurt was fused with anger when he spoke.

"And today, you give me your ass to kiss."

Oh My God, what have I done? Sarah thinks to herself, but remains silent and very scared still.

Jason slowly walks to the closet of the guest bedroom and emerges with a wrapped package, about 15 inches tall, a few inches wide and very heavy. "Open it," he demands as he hands it to her, tears beginning to stream down his face again, but the look on his face is almost emotionless, but slight hints of anger sit at the corners of his lips.

She slowly unravels the paper on the package and reveals a black, shiny glazed sculpture of a beautiful woman, dressed in a long, flowing gown. On her arm she wore a sparkly, silvery object. It was a woman's ring – a diamond and platinum engagement ring, to be exact. She sat there, staring, stunned.

"The statue of the woman is supposed to be YOU. I made that statue of you with my bare hands and my intense love for you in my heart, at the university craft studio. I didn't want you to know that I was doing this, I wanted to surprise you. That ring was your engagement ring – I wanted to spend the rest of my life with you, grow old with you, have my offspring by you, and have you help me nurture them into maturity. You were the soulmate I had been seeking all my life, and I wanted the world to know you were MY wife, for life."

"How could you afford this ring? Where did you get the money for this?" Sarah gasped, still in shock and awe.

"Do you remember two weeks ago when I asked you to come with me for the reading of my parents' will, the attorney had finally found it after all these months?" Jason began. "And your company had you fly to San Francisco the night before and you couldn't accompany me? Well, it turned out that even though my parents didn't have much, they did have a house and a $50,000 life insurance policy, and it was to be split evenly between me and my brother. Patrick died along with them, so I am the only living beneficiary in their will. So I now possess a house and the money – both of which I planned to surprise and share with YOU at dinner tomorrow night – and finally have you spend some time with ME, take time off and not have to work so hard. On top of that, I was going to ask you to MARRY me, be my wife for life, let you relax for once."

"But it seems that I am the one who got the REAL surprise, huh Darlin'?"

With that statement, Jason took the statue and the ring gingerly out of Sarah's hands. He removed the ring, and while staring at her, tears streaming down his face, with hurt and fury burning in his eyes, he dropped the ring in his shirt pocket. He then took the statue, kissed and stroked it tenderly, then threw it with all his might against the stone wall on the other side of the room, shattering the statue into a million sharp bits and shards on the other side of the room, littering the carpet below.

Sarah watched this whole scene in silent shock, brokenhearted, disoriented and terrified as to what he would do next.

Jason turned toward Sarah. Immense hurt, pain, disappointment and disillusionment shone on his tear-stained face. He stared at her a long moment. "We've wasted our time with each other, Sarah. If you could say those words to me, then you never really knew me. I am sorry for that. Good-bye, Sarah," he said, and started walking toward the door, tears streaming down his face once again.

"NO JASON! WAIT, PLEASE! I DO LOVE YOU, I ALWAYS HAVE LOVED YOU!" screamed Sarah as she rushed to stop Jason from leaving. She reached him, threw her arms around him and started crying uncontrollably.

Jason turned back toward her. "Mere words do not affect me. But the context in which they are given certainly does. And the message from you was VERY clear. In effect, you *believe* I am a lazy bum who does nothing for you. You took care of me as if I were some sort of pet, and you derived very little pleasure or meaning out of it. You flipped the script somewhere along the line and did not tell me Darlin', and you left my ass flapping in the wind, pretending everything is all right and living in my own fantasy world. Tell me I am wrong about what you were thinking... Tell me!"

"Jason..." she started to say, but she couldn't say a thing. He was absolutely right.

"And I refuse to marry a woman who feels that way about me. Now take your hands off me and let me go," said Jason, a hint of venom in his voice.

Sarah was taken aback, and she knew he meant it, so she reluctantly let him go. He turned, began walking away and she watched helplessly from her doorway as he finally disappeared from view.

She could hear the silence as her heart broke in a million little pieces, falling to the very depths of her being, as her future had just done against her living room wall.

'SHE COULD HEAR THE SILENCE'
Part IV - Janae
(Excerpt #3 from upcoming novel by RM Green)

Newly divorced Janae didn't feel like going home to her empty house yet, especially since her kids were at her Mom's until next week, so she sat listening to the soft mellow jazz performed by the quartet onstage. Besides, her eye had been on this particular guy ever since he walked into the club. It was time to start emerging from the rubble of her failed marriage and start living. Feeling bolder than usual since she had a few drinks under her belt, and knowing her friends were now gone, she decided that there was no time like the present.

The physical wounds had long since healed, but the mental scarring was still fresh in her mind. Janae yearned to be tenderly held by a man, to have a man's touch bring her to the plateau of physical ecstasy rather than have his touch bring hurt and pain, which she was so used to and had endured for many years. She needed to feel like a woman again. Could this stranger make that happen for her, make her feel alive again? For just one night?

Muscular, toned and striking, with chocolate caramel skin and built like a football running back, he caught her eye right away – she loved muscular men! His dark eyes sparkled and his lips looked sumptuous as he sipped his drink, standing in a far corner for most of the night. She purposely stared at him to make sure he KNEW she was looking at him. She hoped he would come join her at her table. After a few minutes he finally looked her way and they made eye contact. She felt her body tingle with excitement. She couldn't help it, but she caught herself licking her lips after she gently bit her lower lip as he returned her gaze. Her heart started pumping hard and fast when he started walking toward her.

"Would you like to dance?" he asked.

"Sure" she said as he took her hand gently in his and led her to the small but crowded dance floor. The quartet was playing "*For The Love of You*" by the Isley Brothers, and he pulled her close to his body as they started to sway to the music. His touch, his smell and the firmness of his body felt amazing – it had been a long time since a man held her like this.

"Um…you feel so good," he murmured in her ear.

'My sentiments exactly!' Janae thought to herself.

"What is your name?"

"Janae," she answered softly. "And yours?"

"Derek," he answers in a low husky whisper.

Just then she began to feel him press his body closer to hers and felt as though she might lose her mind. She felt his breathing become more ragged. Derek pulled her even closer and kissed her gently on the neck. She felt raw sexual energy building, rising within her.

They continued to dance to the slow, sensual beat of the music, until they were both at a fever pitch and could no longer contain their passion for each other.

Janae attempted to rationalize why she should allow this stranger to use her body for his pleasure. But in all actuality, she would really be using him. *I just want to - NEED to - feel good again – oh please let him take me to ecstasy...*

Ecstasy was a very rare feeling indeed during her long, torturous decade-long marriage to Greg.

She had met Greg seven years ago during a customer service seminar at the University of Maryland, just after landing a CSR position at Riggs National Bank in DC. During the lunch break, while she was quietly eating a tuna sandwich on a croissant and pasta salad, reading through some of the seminar material, he approached her table.

"Is anyone sitting here?" Greg asked politely.

"No, you can sit there," Janae answered politely but disinterested.

"Thank you," he said then sat down.

They sat eating silently for a several minutes, he gazing at her while she read and ate. She never looked up and pretended to not notice or feel him staring at her, but she was very much aware of it. She just didn't feel like making small talk, and she couldn't wait until this thing was over so she could go home and get some sleep. Working days and attending night classes had worn her to a frazzle.

"Greg Pierce here," he finally said, extending his hand.

"Janae Wilson," she says reluctantly, returning his handshake.

He tightened his grip on her hand and held it, forcing her to stare back at him angrily while trying to yank her hand away.

"What do you think you are *doing*?" Janae angrily demanded.

"Just as I suspected," he replied. "You have the most beautiful eyes I have ever seen!"

Janae's anger and defenses quickly melted away at the compliment, replaced by pleasure from his flattery. After a long moment she finally took her hand back from his, and muttered a meek "Thank you."

"What were you reading so intently?" Greg asked.

"Just some material from the seminar. You should have the same thing. Where's yours?" she asked.

"Back on the table in the meeting room where I was sitting," Greg answered. "I never really look that closely at that stuff. I come to these seminars for three reasons; they get me out of the office, the credits for these things look good on my resume, and the BOSS is paying for it all!"

"Yes, I guess you have a point there," Janae answered. They continued getting acquainted over lunch.

She joined him at his table after lunch was over, making small talk throughout. After the seminar he took her to dinner at Ruby Tuesday's near the Capitol Center.

It was a whirlwind courtship. He seemed to worship the ground she walked on, and showered her with gifts and phone calls daily. She was swept off her feet. Two months after the seminar, Janae became Mrs. Pierce and moved into Greg's home.

Unfortunately, so did Dr. Jekyll and Mr. Hyde.

Things started to change almost immediately after their marriage, and intensified as time went on. He quickly persuaded her to drop out of college and start a family – he wanted to take care of his family himself, and insisted that he didn't need any help. He decided she needed to be at home and take care of the kids, so after she became pregnant with Savannah, he insisted that she quit her job at the bank. Two and a half years later, Greg Jr. came along.

Janae began feeling more and more like a prisoner. There was only one car – Greg claimed they couldn't afford two on his salary - so when Greg went to work, she was stuck in the house all day with the kids and without a car, in a rural part of Wheaton. He called her six, seven or more times a day, and when he couldn't reach her, he got an angry, even jealous, attitude, which he normally took out on her once he got home. The terms "fat whore", "stupid bitch", and "you can't do anything right" began regularly peppering his vocabulary when he spoke to her.

Greg couldn't stand any of her friends, so she slowly stopped socializing with them, and called them very infrequently. He didn't get along with her family either, so she slowly began withdrawing from them as well, for fear of triggering Greg's wrath. Both her friends and family loathed Greg, and prayed that Janae would wake up and find the strength to leave him. They found themselves powerless over Greg's unrelenting hold on her.

Once, when Janae refused to make love to him, he came from the kitchen with a knife and held it to her throat while he raped her. That event prompted her to leave him the first time.

He begged and pleaded for her to come back to him, with promises of change while showering her with gifts, and she eventually gave in. For a short while, things changed for the better. But within weeks Janae found herself back in the same oppressive situation again, which continually worsened as time went on. Nothing she ever did was good enough – there was almost no pleasing him.

The abuse escalated. Over the ensuing months and years, she was thrown down the short flight of stairs that lead from the living room to the kitchen because dinner was late; slammed against the living room wall and slapped for paying the telephone bill one day late; punched in the face for giving an attractive male directions to Wal-Mart while they walked down the road; she lost two side teeth from a right punch across her jaw for going shopping with a girlfriend without his permission; she was regularly denied sleep from Greg's all-night tirades; he even punctured her right breast with a screwdriver on another occasion during which he raped her. He always said the same thing, like a broken record - she 'made him do' all these things to her, and if she would 'just do what he said', everything would be fine. She'd heard it so much she'd begun to believe it. Her self-esteem was near zero.

For some strange reason, she still loved him. She'd left him a total of five times, running to friends & family eager to help. Each time they would helplessly watch him would woo her back, with promises of changing and 'getting help', only for her to find after a few weeks she'd been fooled once again. She always went back because of the kids; they needed him and they would miss him, and she loved him still. But SOMETHING had to be done – she could not go on living like this. She had to talk to him and make him listen to reason.

"Greg, why do you hit me and call me names all the time? When we have problems, we can work things out without all that."

"Hell, don't you know that's how I show you I love you, by keeping you in line?" he answered. "That was the way it was around my family's house. Dad spoke and we jumped, especially Momma, and he loved her. Momma worshipped him. I'm being NICE to you compared to Daddy. I didn't like it when Mom had to go to the hospital, and you've hardly had to go. Just do as I say and we have no problems."

"Well, I can't live like this anymore, Greg. I've got to go," Janae replied. Greg turned to look at her, with dark fury in his eyes.

"You ain't going NOWHERE with MY kids, Bitch!" He grabbed her by her throat and began squeezing until she was beginning to choke. "And if you try it, I will hunt you down and kill YOU and THEM, you understand me woman? If I can't have you, NO ONE ELSE WILL!"

She KNEW what that meant.

The next morning after he went to work, Janae called her friend Monica, who had information on domestic violence shelters that Greg didn't know anything about. After Greg called Janae from work the first time, and she was satisfied he was at work almost an hour's drive away, she packed a few days' clothing, picked up Savannah and Greg Jr. from school, and called the domestic violence shelter from there. After a short telephone interview, she was accepted into the shelter and they were whisked away to the safe house by police car from the school.

When Greg found out she was gone, he grew angry and desperate, calling everyone he knew to try to find her and coax her back again. Janae only shared her plans with Monica, who would never tell Greg. She too had lived through domestic violence, and knew Janae needed to save her life as well as the lives of her children.

During their few weeks at the shelter, Janae and the kids received counseling. She found out through the children's counseling sessions that the kids were HAPPY that their parents broke up – they felt the tension and the violence in the house. They were terrified of their father, but even more afraid that Greg would hurt their mom.

She prayed and thanked God for her blessings; she and the kids had finally achieved a certain measure of peace of mind. Even Greg, with whom she had extremely limited contact, appeared to be a changed man, having begun anger management sessions on his own volition. The shelter arranged free legal counsel for Janae, and she was awarded not only temporary possession of their home, but a restraining order to keep Greg away from the house. Since she still had no job, the court ordered for him to continue paying the bills.

As it turned out, Janae didn't need the restraining order after all. Greg had found another woman (whom she later found out he had been sleeping with for over two years prior to their separation), ran off to Florida with her and basically abandoned them, a common occurrence with men who commit violence. When a woman fights back, they often retreat. Janae was determined to support herself and her children, and found a good job after working as a temp for some months. Her new life was beginning to take shape. God was answering her prayers.

And now she needed a physical manifestation of the end of her battered and bruised past. She knew it was wrong in God's eyes to be with a man she wasn't married to. However the overwhelming physical and emotional pain of the past ten years with Greg had to be put to rest.

After the song was over, Janae and Derek left the club and went around the corner to a nearby hotel, and Derek paid for a room.

Once behind the locked door they could barely contain the burning passion that had built up on the dance floor. They started kissing passionately, licking and sucking on each other's lips, neck and chest while their hands explored each other's bodies.

Janae was dripping wet as Derek ran his fingers over the thin material of her panties, which excited and pleased him all the more. She let out deep moans as his touch sought then brushed against her clitoris, her body bucking and reacting to his touch. Derek kept stroking her until she felt her body begin shaking, then climaxing, oozing her wetness all over his fingers. When Janae finally finished her much-needed and sought after orgasm, she took his fingers into her mouth, then licked and sucked her own juices off them. She pushed him back on the bed and whispered, "It's my turn, now. Just relax and let me please you."

Janae began undressing him, kissing every part of him as she slowly removes each piece of clothing, taking special care to suck his nipples and lick his body down to his navel. She removed his pants and licked her lips as she savored the view of his hard throbbing penis.

She began to strip for him, slowly removing her blouse, then her bra. She sensuously swayed to soft music coming from the radio on the night stand, and began to pinch and play with her nipples, making them hard and rigid. Derek watched her mesmerized, his longing to take her barely containable. She leisurely shimmied out of her skirt, and then slowly removed her panties to reveal her dripping wetness; the hair of her vulva glistening with desire for him. She inserted one finger, then two, into her vagina, and then had Derek watch her masturbate herself to another orgasm.

Derek's manhood stood straight up in the air, precum oozing out the tip. She knelt in front of him and licked up the salty-sweet, sticky liquid. She gently flicked the tip of her tongue all around the head of his penis, as deep moans of pleasure slipped from Derek's lips, his eyes rolled in the back of his head, and he closed his eyes to fully absorb the the ecstasy of his entire world being reduced to feel of her tongue on the head of his cock. She slowly sucked on the head, taking just a little more in her mouth with each suck until she can't take in any more. She nibbled all the way up and down the shaft as she pumped him with her hand, hearing him moan and feeling his body rock beneath her. She ran her tongue over his testicles and drew them into her warm mouth one by one, gently sucking on them, almost taking him over the edge.

Oh no, he can't cum yet, I must feel him inside me, Janae thought. She straddled him, rubbed her dripping pussy against his cock, and then lowered her vagina onto his rock hard, throbbing penis…

"Whose cock is this, Derek? Tell ME!" Janae demanded.

"It's yours Janae, it's your cock, Baby, all yours!" he moaned, over and over again.

And Janae rocked her body harder, up and down, more intensely each time he says her name. She was about to reach climax when he flipped her over on the bed and entered her from behind. He pulled her hair firmly but erotically, and pumped her vagina hard, grabbing her hips to go deeper, as deep as he can, hitting bottom...

"Now tell ME whose pussy this is!" Derek demanded.

"It's yours Derek, all yours!" Janae half screamed/half moans each time he asks. Just then she felt him shoot his cum inside her vagina as he loudly groaned, his body shaking, his penis throbbing inside her. She began climaxing again, her body trembling as she collapsed on the bed. He rolled off of her, completely spent.

They pulled each other close, their bodies still gleaming from sweat and hot, raw, passionate sex. Cuddling under the covers, they fell into a deep sleep, wrapped in each other's arms.

My body needed this, she thought to herself. Derek was sweet revenge for all the pain, anguish, tears and scars she endured during her 10 years with Greg, now symbolically conquered.

Janae awoke a few hours later, still feeling elated from last night, but she also knew that she simply needed release and closure of her past life. Now that she had crossed into a new day, over a new threshold, she could begin living again. She looked over at the still sleeping Derek, and silently thanked him for the newfound strength he had no idea he just provided her.

Quietly but swiftly, she gathered her clothing scattered about the room. She could hear the silence racing in her mind as she looked at his sleeping figure, and felt immense gratitude for what he'd done for her. She dressed, kissed Derek softly on the forehead, left a yellow rose, which she had plucked from flower vase in the room, on the empty pillow. She softly whispered 'Thank You" to Derek. She then closed the door softly as she left the hotel for home.

She would never see him again.

If you or someone you know is in an abusive relationship, please contact your local domestic abuse shelter or go to www.ncadv.org to find help in your area. You could save a LIFE!

Terance Williams

"Just Yesterday I was going thru a rough time, and a possible low point in my life. You see, I am not an overly religious person, but I do believe in the power of prayer. I closed my eyes, grabbed a pen and this is what flowed from it. Hope It Helps someone as much as it helped me."
Terance 'Easy Tee' Williams

WILL MONEY MAKE YOU HAPPY?

I've been unhappy for so long,
and I've spent many a day-
wondering just where I went wrong,
do I turn left? go right?
or just accept defeat.
Do I feel bitter, & heartbroken,
That my life is not sweet?
wondering if I still have the catlike-
ability to land on my feet?
Would money make things better?
Will it make my life appear together?
Can it make someone love me?
And will it last forever?
Will it give me power-respect?
Will having it make me lust?
Or just create, greed abuse and distrust?
Heaven knows I seen it make some kill!
So-
If it's in GOD WE TRUST-
Why is it printed on a bill?
Answer is I don't know, and
truth is I don't care;
"But please, OH PLEASE LORD!!!"
HEAR AND ANSWER MY PRAYER!
Lord, help me out of this-financial bind-
shower me with your light,
so I am no longer blind,
It's not about greed,
Its about need-NOT DESIRE,
It's about
protecting your children,
& proving the Devil a Liar.
I need your hand, even the tip
of your finger,
to touch all of those I love-
and show those - that do not
know your POWER.
So They too may rise above....

May All Of You Be Blessed,
Share it with those in need.

written by:
Terance "EASY TEE" Williams
Street Legal Entertainment
BRM Music Group
easytee.streetlegalent.com

Noah
Travis

Br0tha'z.....

Dam, can a young brotha live ? Please !
At least til 30, so i could get a lil more time with my kidz......
How bout 40 or 50 ?
Thatz a good length of time, f0r a y0ung br0tha today......
I dont caRe what nobody say......
Im only going by what i see -
Not trying 2 rush death my way.....
Itz 4 eternal life i pray.........
But n0t on this earth -
for with the m0st high, i'll be one day !!
They say, that t0day, a y0ung br0tha gotta pack that steel....
If he wantz 2 lessen the chance, of his own blood spill.......
But, i kn0w that's a lie !!
Caus i don' seen hommiez, that had machine gunz die...........
Or get life in the pen.......
wich meanz , that gun fight, he still didnt win..........
and then, itz hard just tryin 2 stay outta this mess......
To keep GOD, WISDOM, and PRAYER az ya GUNZ, iz ya best bet !!
But yet, d0nt get me wr0ng.......
I think there iz a time 2 pick uP tha kr0m' ......
but only 2 pr0tect ya family and h0me..........
I bend my kneez, and pray
that the'll never c0me a day,
that in selfdefense i'll have 2 sla' ,
one of my own -
Br0tha'z......

www.myspace.com/noahtravis

A POEM FOR HER

itz p0rin rain,
az she standz there under an umbrella,
with eyez that sayz, 4ever in deep th0ughtz....
and a smile, that fr0m that day....
shall 4ever grip my heaRt.......
i stand, and stare fr0m a distance,
struggling 2 lo0k away.........
thinkin that s0mthin s0 beautiful,
has 2 bel0ng 2 GOD himself........
and i just d0nt wanna get in tha way.......
s0 i'll just walk past, tip my hat,
and keep that white r0se behind my back.......
and walk back 2 yesterday -
and thank GOD, 4 sh0win me that tha sun can shine
even on dark dayz.........

n0ah - Copyright 2004. All Rights Reserved.

www.myspace.com/noahtravis

Felecia
Trotter

Poem 1

Did I sign a living will
To live in hell on earth?
Was it not enough that my mother struggled in pain
To give me birth?

Living in a world of freedom
Patronized by your fist
Droplets from soft eyes
Twisted, full of mist

Strong hands, that vowed to hold me
Only to scold me, full of rage
Demanding to always be on center stage
Performance was to tear me down
Silently I sat, never saying words
Too scared to make a sound

Around others I faked a smile, once in a while
Till you determined that was a sin
And your fists had to win
So the silence again would begin

"Just be quiet" you need to stay alive
My children are watching
For them, I must survive

Did I sign a living will
To live in hell on earth?
Was it not enough that my mother was in pain
To give me birth?

It's easy to give up
It simply requires "nothing"!
I was determined my silence would sing

Family was the corner stone
To regain my sanity
Liberty
My dignity

On my knees, I spoke to God

I made a plea
He opened my eyes
Blessed me to see
Exactly what "He"
Had planned for me

Poem 2

I've seen and felt enough pain
to live these 48 years all over again
The deception, betrayal, beatings and games
I love myself so much right now
but once, I didn't feel the same

Things were tough
but I made it
I'm a survivor
and still "I love"............regardless

More than one is at fault
for past memories I regret
for I must be honest
and confess

I blamed another for pain and abuse
but it was I who accepted
being at your disposal
for any and all your use

Things were rough
But I made it
I'm a survivor
and still "I love"...........regardless

Finally at that stage
Re-tired
children said "no more mama"
they knew I had
Been-tired

Now on to a new phase
how to relax
mind set to jump
just my normal reflex

I made it
I survived
So please understand
and take me by both my hands
look me in my wet tired eyes
and see what I see

A wonderful you
and I
racing toward the future
shouting back to all the past
a last and final

good-bye

The Promise

I had a conversation with my daughter today
We talked of when our Father calls me to come his way
I have three beautiful children, and four wonderful grands
Therefore I want seven spectacular doves
To represent my undying love

To fly high above this earth with me
As I graciously float above

My daughter said "Mom we live in the hood"
"We only have black crows"
Look high in the trees
Perched upon the wood

But I'm not worried, she'll grant my request
My children have always treated me their best
And they would want their mom
To be at peace and rest

So release my seven doves
And my babies, try not to cry
You know if your love could have saved me
I never would have died

Release our love into the sky
As we say our earthly good-bye
As I'm laid into the dirt
I promise to always

Always

Take on all

Your hurt

7/6/2007

Jason Tucker

~ My People ~

I am a white man
The legacy of a long line
Of white men

My people drop the bombs, not yours

I can't help that
I would dispel the curse
Of this skin I was born with

My people enslaved the black man, not yours

I know that no matter what I do
People will make assumptions
Based on the color of my skin

My people stole America, not yours

I know the history of my people

And that, my friend, will never go away

My people burn crosses, not yours

Amused by thoughts of supremacy
At the expense of lost innocents

My people incited the holocaust, not yours

Aroused by the pain of other races
And set to bathe in their sorrow

My people are the oppressors, not yours

I listen and wonder
What would spik, chink, fag, and nigger
Really mean in a perfect world

My people invented racial slurs, not yours

It doesn't help that I know
I didn't do any of that
It'll never change the fact

It is my skin that makes me nervous, not yours

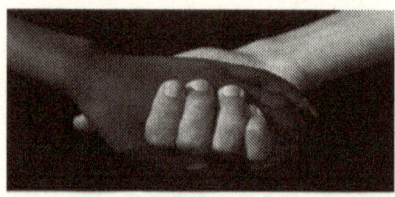

~

Jason Tucker, Copyright @ 2007. All Rights Reserved.

~ Love Within ~

Dreams venture to lands where we belong
together sharing intimacy as defined
by our bodies combined at your
welcoming hips and those
beautiful lips. Sensual
endless bliss. The
best in all of
creation.
You.
Desire
inspires a most
hormonal inferno where
fires shall create this lovely
moment in time together nude
and longing for a taste of
one another's nectar
to quash need
of hunger.
Love me.
use me, be one
with my core. venture
with me to love and longing
and fulfill lustful prophecies with
me in mutual convalescence.
Heal me, save me from
poisons the mind
exudes for I
Will love
you
and
forever
it shall be
written to
immortalize
etched in blood
seeping penmanship for
all to see and agree that there's love
within me. Love cast upon a soul
whom envelops my senses in
dreams I extol. Just so far
from my eager grasps.
I gasp to find my
Love at last.
It's you.
<3
~

~ Writer's Array ~

Confined in my imprisoned mind
For entire weekends at a time
Plagued by this current occupation
This writer's fueled by his frustration

Set free by love bestowed upon me
Though secret, whom is plain to see
Imbued with the words by god's greatest creation
This writer's fueled by his adoration

Seeking enlightenment and pushing myself
To learn and attain knowledgeable wealth
To press forward in rhyme and dictation
This writer's fueled by education

The feelings I scribe all reside inside
This poet. This man who no longer shall hide
For I am your open book for your oration
This writer's fueled by every ovation

The pressing of lips and sexual splendor
Often influence the words that I render
For I, like all of you, enjoy the sensation
This writer's fueled by perverse temptation

Sinks teeth in the blood of any who warrant
Punishment from the God of War: The Abhorrent
To speak unkindly invokes my predation
This writer's fueled by refutation

When life comes to call through my subject matter
It's intent is to charm through my lovely chatter
Thus bringing the reader closer to my realization
This writer's fueled by your gratification

When lost for words even then I will shine
By flipping that material into written line
And reversing the trends of lyrical cessation
This writer's fueled by his own narration

For my readers and friends I shall strive to perform
At the standard of your expectations with poems so warm
And heartfelt to touch each of you in any situation
This writer's fueled by his obligation

And it's all for your admiration

I love you all, you're my illumination

~

~ Love Letter ~

When the street lights come on
I am driven to you every night
longing for your embrace and
approval. To have you listen
and talk to me like a dearest
friend. With me till the end
of my journey and cheering
once I cross the threshold, the
pinnacle of any such race. To
encourage me to be a winner
and lavish me with kind words
expelled from sweetest lips
of confections. Appreciated
to no end for all of your minor
exceptions and shortcomings
combined in one beautifully
gift wrapped package with
a cutesy little bow on the top.
Loved and respected in all
sincerity since virtually the
first time we met. I was in
love in a far out kind of way
and there was indeed no way
for me to hide it from you so I decided to write it all down for you.
You are the drive that dwells within my mind of affections and
for that I must say thank you. This testament I write for you
is written with a pen leaking blood and compassion in
to fine pools on a wonderful canvas on display for
the whole world to see and realize the extent
of my undying passion to pleasure you.
I am all yours for the love you
Dispense upon me in a
cascading pour.
I love you
reader
<3
~

Timothy Hollins

Mississippi Voodoo/Mississippi Mirrors

Lies smear my mirror; voodoo thoughts thinking
Can potions be it? I, myself, sip on tonics
Crawdads in ditches; riverbeds with fool wishes
Down that ole Mississippi, folklore pours
And that evil old lady sprinkling powder at my door
Is it that she's confused, or am I conned and fused with old ways
Thick humid days we try and cut with dull blades
I'm so stuck in my ways
I'm so stuck in clay muds baked onto a page
Sitting high in cream skies till our dreams wither and fade
This is how we see hope
Us good ole country folk, faith included
On the front porch seduced with moonshine and blues
Him over there; so far from me too
So he thinks esoteric, hants and spirits
Three-headed witch doctors to mind states so weary
And then these noted doctors sweating vodka over births
Either way we're cursed in my mirror
So I see with closed lips and talk with blind eyes
And ride the mental planes into horrific skies
In order to maintain, and walk with some pride
My mirrors reflect nothing but their lives; their lies

Wheels, Wills; Rims, Realms

Travel, destinations; priced or priceless
Opportunist live limits; die rare limitless
Can you dream broken lines seen as portals?
What unknown realms past the will of mortals
Focusing on wheels; enslaved by rims
Who desire the will to cross over a realm?
Which have we succumb to, lost but we ride
Convert convertibles when winds control the time
The disguise; I discuss the years of disgust
Wind blowing in the eyes and minds of us
Centuries of dust polluting the ignorant
Transmitting arrogance, planets laugh from this
Will it pass over us? Distant mental Passover
Dark thoughts, the soldiers; mark of the beast controls
But pure as nature on peaked hillsides I will
Dimensions in pods on titanium wheels
I do space and sound and time and me
I see four ways to three as I wake to sleep
I complex the week to complex the weak
And see streets as streaks so I Windex beliefs
Of priced and destinations; come travel the priceless
Wheels or will, rims or realms I guess
Hidden choices confess that we're lost and not knowing
Minerals build materials that is destroying my people

Short Story
(Book Excerpt)
By
Timothy Hollins,
Author of the novel,
'SACRED GROUND'

'SACRED GROUND' Book Excerpt (Short Story)
By Timothy Hollins

A sea of painful thoughts and black emotions lie just beneath the surface of Joseph Reed, Jr., a young man who has recently been driven to the point of insanity, as he lingers on a gripping tale of hell's demons told by one of his co-workers. Joseph now envisions, in detail, the horrific accounts, as he struggles between illusion and reality. His sanity fades, allowing him to be haunted by the shadowed images he's projected in his mind and the faint sounds that whisper with the night's wind.

This particular night the winds are strong. The naked branches of the trees close to his home scrape continuously against the dining room window. Shadows from the branches create ghostly figures through the thin, lace curtains that blow wildly from the opened window, and the sounds from the night startle him with their rapid untimely movement. He sits at the dining room table - as he does each night - in solitude. But tonight is different. Tonight, he is accompanied by fear. The seconds are suspended as Joseph raises a polished .45 caliber automatic pistol to his head and slowly squeezes the trigger. The darkness inside of him has been freed and so, too, has Joseph.

The next morning arrives quickly as if to anticipate someone finding the lifeless body -as if this body is a close friend of the dawn. The sun shines through the dining room curtains, but its rays are interrupted by a death that will go unnoticed for days. Joseph was somewhat of an introvert, and his social life consisted of sitcoms and frozen TV dinners.

The Friday night suicide soon turns into a Monday morning corpse, and no one has noticed Joseph's absence from work except his secretary. He had instructed her earlier last week to give him morning wake up calls. She dutifully complied. When she called his house Friday and didn't get a response, she figured he might have taken the day off, so she wasn't concerned. She called again first thing Monday morning, but Joseph never answered. Tuesday morning arrived and so did the secretary's call. Still no response from Joseph.

Days earlier, he had informed her of a disturbing phone call he received. The caller threatened his life, and Joseph had no idea who the person was. She remembered him being so rattled from the call that he left the office early that day. Now his body lay breathless.

Morning suns have come and gone since Friday. The body lies limp across the kitchen table, and a terrible stench from the corpse has blanketed the entire house. The Tuesday morning sunrays are strong. The heat carries the foul scent of dried blood and partially exposed brains outside the home. As the sun shines directly onto Joseph's slouched body, one would think the beauty of the light intends to give him life once again.

As the secretary calls, his body lies breathless in a pool of dried blood. She becomes a bit concerned after not being able to reach him by phone. She knows it is unlike Joseph to miss several days of work. All he had was his work. She continues to try to reach him, until her concerns turn to fear. She calls 911.

Police arrive at the house within minutes of the call. They have been informed of the secretary's concerns. The two officers talk casually as they walk up the squeaky wooden stairs continuing the conversation they'd started over morning coffee and glazed doughnuts. They knock several times with no response. The demeanor of the officers quickly changes, as they become aware of the odor. They alert headquarters that they are about to forcefully enter the home.

Kicking twice on the door, it tumbles inward. The smell of the corpse floods their nostrils. The officers, overtaken at first by the awful smell, regain their composure and enter the house. They reach the dining room and find Joseph's body with the .45 automatic still clinched tightly in his left hand.

At the police station, work is underway to inform all immediate kin of the tragic incident. Captain Staps, commander of Precinct 3, assigns his leading detective to the case, Detective Telisha Austin. Austin, a native of Mississippi, had recently been working in San Diego where she was swamped with homicide cases. Not only had she graduated top of her class at the academy, but she also received an expert medallion in marksmanship. The detective had moved to Mississippi only a few weeks prior in hopes of escaping the big city life. She had grown tired of the over-populated cities in California and wanted to regain a "good ol' country life." A life she remembered to be a lot less
strenuous.

"I need answers, Austin!" the captain demands, as he throws the case file on his desk. "And I needed them like two hours ago. I gotta have something to tell this poor bastard's family."

About The Authors

Terance Williams

Born in New York City, Mr. Williams grew up in Harlem and the Bronx, surrounded by the new sounds of rap during it's birth, counting among friends the likes of Cool Herc, Melly Mel, Kurtis Blow and DJ Theodore, among others. He's kept his music close to his heart all his life, and is currently involved with the management of Street Legal Entertainment, headquartered in Baltimore, MD. Mr. Williams has written short stories and poetry on and off throughout his life, and his heartfelt gritty street style shines through.

The proud father of three children now resides in Florida with his wife, Coretta.

~~~~~~~~~~~~~~~~~~~~~~~~~~~~~~~~~~

Noah Travis

Growing up in the mean streets of South Central Los Angeles, Mr. Travis has seen the best and the worst of humanity as he navigated his way through life. His use of words have a way of making even the most mundane occurrence beautiful, romantic and poetic, and his unique style of prose resonates through his work. This writer's poetry comes from the heart, and never ceases to stir the soul.

Still a lifelong resident of Los Angeles, the proud father of two sons is currently working on producing a collection of his own works.

Timothy Hollins

Timothy Hollins has been writing literary works for over 20 years. His love for mystery and science fiction inspired him to write his current novel, Sacred Ground. Hollins currently resides in Atlanta, Georgia and has a beautiful teenage daughter.

Synopsis: The story surrounds Detective Austin, a well-learned and decorated detective in San Diego, California, who decides to move back to her native state; Mississippi. She's assigned to the suicide case of Joseph Reed Jr., a local businessman labeled introvert that comes from a prominent family in Arielleville. While trying to tie-up loose ends to the case, Austin is quickly engulfed in a bizarre investigation that plots murder, betrayal, kidnapping, and a heated love-triangle that just might jeopardize her entire case.

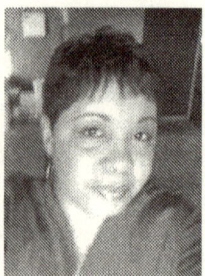

Felecia Trotter

48 year old mother of 3 beautiful children, who have blessed me with 4 wonderful grandchildren. No words can describe the love we share. I have been blessed to be able to retire this year, My children have reversed roles and taken over our family business. Writing has become my way to release and relax. It's a pleasure, a look into my heart and soul.

My motto:

It's nice to be important
But it's important to be nice

Thank you Jesus!

Jason Tucker

Jason Tucker is like poetry fable fusion. Bringing the light to the darkness. Prides himself in his heartfelt "pen's lifeblood". Writing since age 14, he has transcended his boundaries and limitations time and again with a drive and a devotion to raise the bar.

Recently the proud co-creator of a rising poetry forum entitled Wordplay Workshop where he spends his time exposing other writer's to inspiration and creative challenges and contests. "I wanted to give back to the writing community that has embraced me so warmly."

He currently spends a lot of time promoting the works of others. A selfless talent for exposure. A great heart and a magnificent way with rhyme and diction. Please enjoy the works of Jason...

RM Green

Currently this writer is hard at work on her first novel, **'SHE COULD HEAR THE SILENCE'**, a drama which takes a look inside the personal lives of five Black female friends. **Anticipated Publication Date: December, 2007.** She also produces a weekly urban drama/soap opera, **'EVERYBODY PLAYZ THA FOOL'**, on Myspace (http://www.myspace.com/msblaqbuttafly). Formerly wrote short stories for young adults, dealing with such subject matter as homelessness, dating and college life. Major writing influences are Tyler Perry, Terry McMillan, Sidney Sheldon, Alice Walker, John Grisham and Agatha Christie.

Her article, *'Dead In The Water'* appeared in the October 19 - 25, 2006 issues of **Black Conscious News Ezine**. This article portrays a humourous view of the struggle Black 'Baby Boomers' go through trying to find love while balancing family and career. Also, her article *'High Prevalence of Fibroids in Black Women'* is featured in the October 30 - November 3, 2006 issues.

Her poems, *'Shinnecock Dreams'* and *'Warrior Love'* are both featured in the Fall, 2006 issue of **Taborri Press Ezine**. Both poems describe different aspects of Native American life. They are also currently featured in the November, 2006 issue of **Autumn Leaves Ezine**, which is primarily devoted to the poetry and writings of the Native American community. *'Warrior Love'* is also featured in **Sage of Consciousness** ezine, Volume 2 Issue 4, Fall/Winter 2006, which features and celebrates poems, essays, short stories and artwork from a diverse pool of artisans from all over the world.

Currently divorced, she resides in Beaufort, SC with her three daughters.

www.ingramcontent.com/pod-product-compliance
Lightning Source LLC
Chambersburg PA
CBHW021450240626
47154CB00005B/1794